THE HOOK WAS VERY SHARP

ginger lepto
@gmail.
com

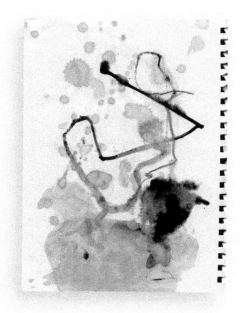

THE HOOK WAS VERY SHARP

GINGER LEGATO

ABIQUIU PRESS

ISBN 978-1-7238237-2-3 (paper)
ISBN 978-1-7328237-3-0 (electronic)

Publised by Abiquiu Press
abiquiupress@gmail.com
First Edition
Printed in the United States of America

for

Francis John Peter

CONTENTS

I want the shelter
    of the doorframe

of a prayer. If only
    for a moment

I want to stand like the blue flame
    of a wave

in a set of waves.

—Michael McGriff, "Cormorants"

THE HOOK WAS VERY SHARP

PRELUDE

RUE

Mourning's reverie

Tongue aflame

Your light receding

Brightness to ash

I

CREEK

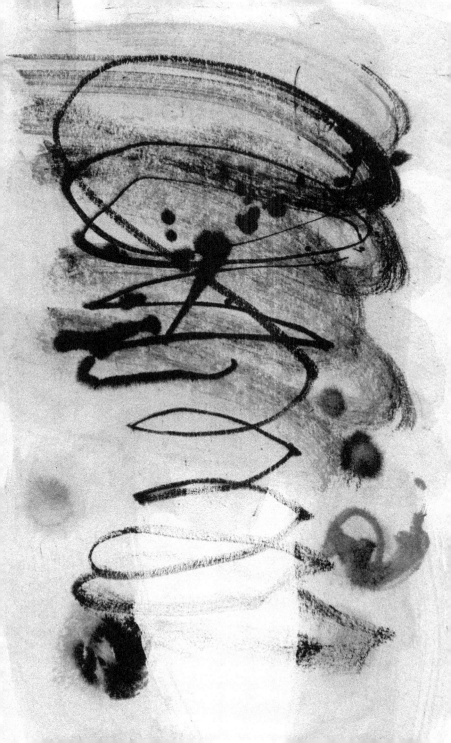

CREEK

O Creek,

where are the speckled trout
where is the man of steel

the poison ivy vines
my gambling man

where are your shallow tadpole pools
my desperado

the black-eyed Susans, skunk cabbage
loser of weekly wages

where are the ruddy tiger lilies
his reforming self

and the blue flag iris
his subtle heart

O Creek,

where is my father?

FAREWELL

What will it be like, Daddy,
plunging my hands into your bones?

I imagine
myself a prizefighter

jab-jabbing, then clinching
your palpable ghost.

Mea culpa. Mea culpa.
I should have gone with you

to Paterson, to Cedar Lawn,
the crematory.

I should have gone down
to the fire chamber

witnessed your burning
fastened the light

of your body
to my own.

Like moth
to flame

seared, refined,
scorched,

curled, cracked,
hollowed out—

a flutter of wings
made elemental.

Instead, I circled
safe and apart

envisioned the oven
reverberation of steel doors

impounding your coffin.
The hiss and roar of flame

consuming
your emaciated limbs.

It would not take long
day would open again

brighten
upon your bones.

    O Creek,

      you have gone dry
      bone-dry.

CREEK

O Creek,

> *where*
> *are my forest guardians*

> *the holy ghost*
> *dogwood trees*

> *the mitt-leafed*
> *American chestnut*

> *my old ones*
> *wise sentinels*

> *mighty fathers*
> *of the wood?*

O Creek,

> *where is my father?*

This private dawn
scrim of night lifting

tendrils of cirrus clouds
sweep the quickening sky.

Puddling light, shaped
like kidneys and livers,

slips into scruff grass
edging the stone pump house

where I place you, Daddy,
sitting legs akimbo

on a wooden-slatted
green folding chair

tilted back against
a cool mossy wall

honey-scented smoke
of Edgeworth tobacco

curling
from your damp burl pipe.

The small, honest, oily pump
ticks and chuffs

as rainwater fills
the ten-foot-square forest pit

owned by your neighbor
who allowed you

to draw water
from his crude well

into your restaurant
for twenty-seven years.

Bullfrogs pose
around the deep wellhole

unruly baritone chorus
quivering with primal language

vibration from the belly
of the deep wood.

We are shades here, Daddy,
crossing time's invisible barrier

dogwoods the lintels
of your heaven

a stone pump house
my passageway to memory.

CREEK

O Creek,

    pebbles of memory cradle
    in my cupped palms

    leaden shoes haul me
    to the ritual of my father's burning

    my offerings are mere sticks
    incense, smoke and ash.

O Creek,

    a child creates the mountain
    the woman ascends its summit.

    Tantus labor non sit cassus
    —so much labor let it not be lost.

II

FISHERMEN

PULSE

We were fishermen
I his tomboy

those summer Mondays
fishermen

threading worms
on fine hooks

the tips of my fingers
laid cold

along the pliant body
of a plump nightcrawler

thick as a ropy vein
in the arm of a wrestler

sinewy, twisting,
bulging,

then narrowing
within my pliered grip.

> *Remember, Creek,*
> *remember the taste of them?*

In the muddled light of morning
he said, they don't feel pain

I said, the hook is very sharp
he said, don't give me that crap

I said, _____ .

SILK

A girl of glass
pressed the barbed shaft

of an Eagle Claw
number 10 hook

into membranous
swollen silk

the cloy scent of the worm
slicked her nostrils.

Stickiness remains
in my fingers' memory

I want to lick them clean
make them reborn.

O Creek,

*if I could tunnel
into damp earth*

*slither into
the nightcrawlers' den*

*on an early pink
summer evening*

*I would apologize.
I glance downward*

your water merciful
deep and calm.

O Creek,

you are singing!

LAMENT

It was November. Night.
The day of the headache.

He was pale, distraught,
whimpering for relief

given pills
that did not help

begging
to go to the hospital.

He hated the hospital—
antechamber

of a terrifying
underworld.

Inside the emergency ward
bleached colorless with illness

we waited
seven hours.

I believed
he was genuinely glad

for my company.
It was the night

of triage, scans, injections,
fluids, blood tests—

an unfamiliar doctor
told me there was bleeding

in the brain
cancer everywhere

they were trying
to find a bed.

I asked
for more blankets.

> *O! Winter father*
> *Holy is your name*
> *Cold hands probe your body*
> *Blood seeping from your brain*

I believed he was genuinely glad
for my company.

Remember I love you, he said
                    —just a little bit.

FAUX

Daddy's cuff links
were not gold after all

some plated alloy
blackened now

peeling badly.
Nonetheless

they enchant me
each time I hold them

childish gift from his
besotted little girl.

A clear glass
half dome on each

holds the bright tiny scene
of a rainbow trout

leaping
from a glinting stream

hooked and dying
on a string.

WOODEN

The fish writhes
in the clutch

of my cold hand.
A delicate yellow perch.

I take the hard back
of your fisherman's knife

like you showed me
swiftly rap the fish's head.

They feel pain,
I tell him,

but do not stop myself
from the killing.

Its body stiffens, wooden
upon my open hand.

I am your fisherman, Daddy,
inhaling the scent of thick blood

wormy odor
mingled with summer heat.

O Creek,

do you heed as I do
the numbed silence of this small death?

KNIFE

Holding Daddy's knife

I am drawn to run my thumb

Along its sharp edge

SLICKER

Remember the big one
I caught

that chilly gray day
sleeves of my slicker

lined against the wind
with the New York *Daily News*?

A young girl
fishing with her father

the stout man
tamping his Dunhill pipe.

I am your special girl
your Monday pal.

Reeling it in with all my strength
not knowing if I had a fish

or if my lure
was caught on trash.

The dockmen knew, watched
the line travel downriver

envied my catch
as I netted it.

An eighteen-inch striped bass
tossing its tail high

glancing
its predator's face.

I asked
if I could keep it.

You said,
it's no good

the river's filthy
throw it back.

I would not believe
my perfect luck

worthless
my prize jettisoned.

You gave in
to my disappointment

we took the fish home
my pride, my trophy,

bringing surplus
to our table that night.

You baked it
with salty butter and herbs

but the taste was bitter.
Iodine. You said,

it tastes like iodine.
My family spat

onto their plates.
We could not eat.

The women
jumped up

cracked eggs
into a sizzling pan—

paltry remedy
for hurt pride.

O Creek,

> *the tug of beauty*
> *hooked on a colorful lure*

> *slammed against*
> *a young girl's yellow slicker.*

CHILL

Crushed bones of cremation

Snuffed fire of my father's body

I plan to cast a fist of you

Into the Hudson River

III

LA FAMIGLIA

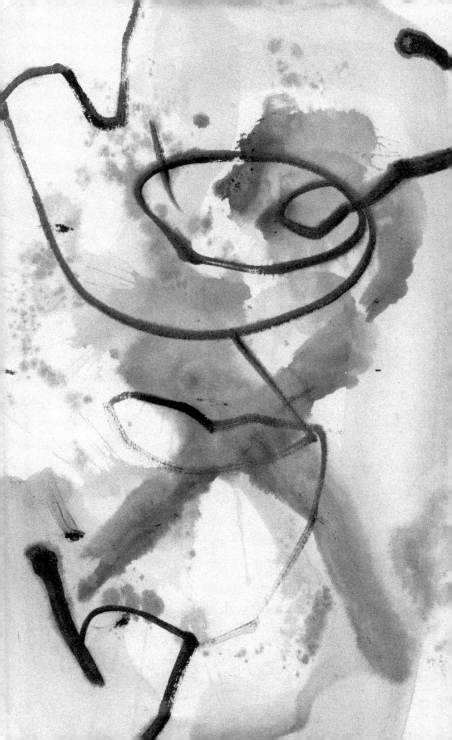

I toss the shuttle of inquiry
across the warp of family history

summon
my father's ghost

invite the phoenix
to rise from his ashes

destroy the bondage
of family indifference

to a girl child's
good fortune.

Daddy, I call to you—
come burn a path

from Hades
to home again

subvert callousness
with mercy.

My pen rekindles the flame
of your passing

words blazing with alchemy
persuading us from rueful darkness.

I dance madly
round and round

a circle of fire
tongue aflame.

We were father-daughter
proud, close to the bone

then broken, broken
by circumstance

each
from
each.

Rise up, Father,
tend your girl child

      I often drown in my dreams

           never fly

              never fly.

LA STREGA

I asked a Wiccan friend
for a spell.

Could she cast anew
Daddy's bad money karma

create prosperity
perhaps cash?

I approach old age
with measly funds

disenchanted
with family lore.

May I? May I please
forgo the legacy

of southern Italian
glum luck?

My Wiccan ally
gave me a list

> jasmine oil   sea salt
> four candles   red thread
> matches for fire
> Daddy's leather wallet
> a few silver coins

she said, write the family names on paper
fold twice—

> *Safino, Legato*
> *Fannelli, Benedetti*
> *Raffaella, Giovanni*
> *Lucia, Vincenzo*
> *Francesco, my father*
> *Teresa, my mother*

you are a chaste vessel of good fortune
wear white linen.

Anoint your forehead
with the jasmine oil of simplicity.

Drink the salty broth
of remembrance and forgiveness.

Barter ties of blood for the cheer
and comforts of your lucky life.

Polish the musty Italian boot
to a high-heeled shine. Dance!

STARDUST

Song-man
crooner—

the lyrics of your favorite song
befit my elegy.

Its tender tune coils in my ear
lifts the clumsy feet of poetry

onto a hotel dance floor.
I twirl these hundreds of words

for you like champagne mixed
with maraschino cherries.

Twilight absorbs your passing
the purple dusk of a dead man's life.

I harbor the reticent ghost
of "Stardust," rescued on the eve

of your nursing-home confinement
when your singing ended.

My slender fingers span the piano keys
dig into Hoagy's dreamy melody

you offered me a *fin* if I could play it right—
Daddy, I am still working on it.

Keep tempo with your daughter
as I impress this poem upon you.

Loneliest of lonely hearts
steadfast father

you are no longer imperiled
by life's indignities.

Neither pawn nor drink
reckless wager, foolish extravagance

will ever again threaten
mother's amethyst ring.

Man of silk—now
you are Luck's Consort.

Our flaws are immeasurable, Daddy,
our frailties precious

I guard my faith in your generosity
in my heart it will remain

I sing your harsh exuberance
without pause.

LIGHT & SWEET

At the breakfast table
he rarely spoke

massaged his brow
pinched the bridge

between his weary eyes
stacked & counted coins

rubber-banded bills
listed supplies

to be purchased
before returning

to his restaurant kitchen
garlicky sauces

clattering pans
thick white dishes.

We sought Daddy's kisses
mother, grandmother & I

tasted his salty
epicurean lips

our family's insistence
for kisses on the mouth.

I resisted the crush
of his beefy arms

hefty frame, the damp
of his sweaty neck

swathed in a triangle
of white handkerchief

tied neatly
with a sailor's knot—

eagerly served him
eggs & toast

coffee
light & sweet.

NANA'S DOELING

Nana raised her fists
above the family circle

shouting, shouting
at you, Daddy,

hurling grievances
her immigrant pain.

Were hers the hardships
that measured your freedom?

You honored your mother
who lived with you

all the years of her life.
Pacified her, casting me

into the tangle
of her cat's cradle—

a surrogate child
for her lost sister, Virginia.

Their mother
dead after birthing

that cherished
precious baby girl.

1918. Influenza. Virginia,
dead at fifteen

I am her namesake
Nana's doeling. Goat girl.

Daddy, you
struck the agreement.

Nana's greedy embrace
pious barbed kisses

her withered affection
a cheerless shroud of longing.

    O Creek,

        have I conformed to her breakage
        am I death warmed over?

FINCHES

Mother and I bought
the finches at Macy's

loveliest
of the captive birds

bright orange beaks
tuxedo feather suits.

Caged at home, they grew
claws unnaturally curled.

Mother cut
the long toenails

too short, the birds bled,
died by morning,

succumbed to her
untaught naive care.

Their stained cage
still sturdy and new

washed clean
was stored away

in the cool basement
where laundry hung

and I claimed
a corner for refuge

concrete walls papered
with magazine racehorses

red roses blanketing
their well-groomed necks.

O Creek,

> *take me to the tiny finches*
> *and to my mother*

> *I will keen and sing*
> *a canticle of tenderness*

> *and contempt*
> *for their bound*

> *and fretful lives.*

BLUSH

Mother shares sixty-six years
of successful marriage

shyly tells me
her secret.

She says,
I never refused him.

At night
in my childhood bed

her moaning
startles me awake

like a rough mantle
pressed against my face.

Gasping for breath
I turn to the pink wall.

IV

WORK

LAST GAS

A fairway of zoysia grass
blankets the wetlands

where Daddy and I
cast our fishing lines

delicate hooks fluttering
like nodding mosquitos

and I waded barefoot
bluegills nipping my ankles.

O Creek!

Sand traps and bunkers
blot your meandering course

surrender-colored pennants
fly from green marker poles

innocent as butterfly wings—
a sight nearly generous enough

to absolve the developers
who create such geography

for plaid-trousered players,
trading stocks, bonds, houses,

kidneys, hearts, weapons,
the blue sky.

O Creek!

Like Daddy's
four acres.

His cozy restaurant
built of local timber

and fieldstones hand-gathered
from the Hudson River Palisades,

the summer hot dog and soda stand,
and the 27 cents a gallon gas station—

bulldozed, flattened, macadamized,
rolled with garish yellow lines

a hundred
tidy parking spaces.

A dazzling STEAKHOUSE logo
now corners the property

where a battered
sheet-metal sign

had announced LAST GAS
to blue-highway travelers.

O Creek!

Winking mini-lights
wrap a few survivor trees

The clamor of party noise
abrades the neighboring forest

leaf, flower, maple, oak
quiver with fatigue

bullfrogs and peepers
no longer sing.

TWELVE BURNER

Twenty-seven years
at the twelve-burner stove

moving like a dancer
ranting at the waitresses.

Dutiful wife on your left
capable assistant.

Eager son
your right-hand man.

Me, shy daughter,
chopping bright vegetables

turning espresso pots
upside down

dolloping whipped cream
onto sweet desserts.

Your old mother circling
like a bird in distress

peregrine
brood hen.

My story renders songs
of sauce and spice

bitter
sweet

flambé, parfait
roux, Mornay.

There at your New Jersey
forest-lodge restaurant

we trained
to be family.

Prepping, cooking,
scraping skillets, pans, dishes

drying silverware with fresh
white tablecloths until 3 a.m.

serving.
     serving.
          serving.

MARTINIS

Daddy liked to tell
the story

about a man
who came to his restaurant

early in the day
sat by the front window

facing the highway
and ordered a double martini.

Suddenly a gasoline tanker truck
rumbled in from the road

parked alongside the restaurant
obstructing the window view—

it was smoking
badly.

The frantic driver jumped
from the truck's cab

ran to the restaurant bar
in search of a public phone

called the volunteer fire department
eleven miles away.

Daddy bellowed
for everyone to leave the place.

Run! Hurry! Mom, take the cash!
Run to the trees!

The man sitting by the window
disregarded the commotion.

Daddy tried to lift his elbow
guide him out to the open air

but the man refused to move
he wanted another martini.

Daddy rushed to the bar
pulled gin and vermouth

from their colorfully lit niches
pounded the bottles

on the man's table
before running for shelter.

We gasped each time
he told that story

his brawny arms raised
voice husky with mischief

laughed and sighed
learning that it was summer

and the truck's radiator
was simply overheating.

My father
bodhisattva of the barroom

heeded the man's despair
chanced life and liquor

giving small comfort
to a traveler

arrived
at the end of his road.

Daddy, you bought
your "little joint on the highway"

in 1944
the year I was born.

Roughly built of wood
and stone

no water, stinky outhouse
fireplace for warmth—

steadily established
your place-hold there

amid skittish
postwar years

worked fifteen hours a day
closed Mondays.

Your acclaimed restaurant
began humbly

offering hot dogs, soda, and beer
finished its run with filet mignon

smothered in artichoke hearts,
shallots, Veneto dry wine.

On the last night of business
you poured vodka

into shot glasses
for all at the bar

toasted your journey
from elevator boy,

cabaret dancer, dock worker
to barman, chef, restaurateur.

Cheers went up!
Everyone shouted, *Down the hatch*!

then tossed their glasses
over drunken shoulders

into the stone-cold
fireplace.

FAREWELL

The skeletal reduction
of my bully-man

came to me
in a tin can.

Crushed shards, ashes
neatly packed

number 51536
punched into the lid.

The container got tucked away
for years, Daddy,

into the catacomb
of a crammed clothes closet

before I could scatter
your earthly remains

upon the foundation stones
of your bygone restaurant

into the Hudson River
where the striped bass spawn

at Belmont Park racetrack
thoroughbreds whinnying

for your losses.

V

LUCK

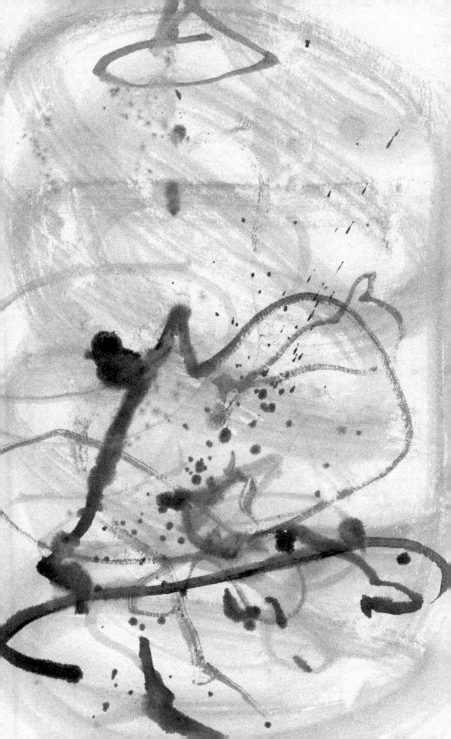

WHAT LUCK?

I am the one
who placed his not-so-lucky

lucky chestnut
into the cardboard coffin.

He had so wanted
to pass it on to me

the hook, the legacy,
his losses, played-out pride.

An auburn chestnut, burnished
with the sweat and oil

of his gambling fist
where dice clicked

then hushed
as he blew on them

before casting the ivories
against green felt.

Seed of his discontent
pressed reverently

into the palm of my hand
as if it were treasure.

For years
I saved your gift, Daddy,

in the top drawer of my dresser
nestled with other cherished items

    mother's platinum
    Bulova watch

    a New Mexico
    turquoise necklace

    coins from Prague
    and Rome

    three gold-capped
    extracted teeth

    the two-dollar bill
    inscribed *Happy Easter.*

Tuck this into his coffin,
I told the funeral director.

Time had come
to nix the jinx.

Let the chestnut
burn with the tree.

SPORT OF KINGS

Close to his dying
I am the sweet-scented talc

dusting his dry arms
his neck, his steel-gray sternum.

Five years later
I dangle my fists

over the rail along the finish line
at Belmont Park racetrack.

The swift winner's head
bowing low at the wire

as I release Daddy's dust
into the bitter, dark,

noble soil
of his addiction.

ASHES

It's Father's day
racing day
Belmont Park opens early

I'm on my way
to a burial
wearing Dad on my hips

his ashes packed
into my pants pockets
close to my body

left pocket
his penknife
a sandwich-size bag of ashes

right pocket
ashes
a twenty-dollar bill

I take the F Train
at Church Avenue
then the N6 bus

drizzling rain
the track will be "good"
buy the New York *Daily News*

check the morning lineup
race 5 number 2
Love My Mondays

my hunch
of the day
that's what I'll play

restaurant
closed on Mondays
Daddy went to the track

racing tips scribbled
on a scrap of folded paper
tucked into his breast pocket

compulsion drove him
like a somnambulist
into his car

onto the New York highways
the blaring racetrack parking lot
then up to the jam-packed grandstand

smelling of greasy hot dogs
mingled with sweat, cigarettes,
horses, and beer

HOT DOGS! I order a jumbo
with mustard relish sauerkraut
and a luscious heady beer

the 5th race comes round and
number 2 Love My Mondays
is the long shot

I feel foolish
playing my hunch
instead bet 1 3 6

override luck's charm
for Daddy's
favorite numbers

AND THEY'RE OFF—a fast start
  they're coming round the half-mile pole
    Love My Mondays moves to the outside >
      she's gaining ground >> Love My Mondays
        in front at the quarter mile >>> she's stretched out
          and into the final furlongs >>>> it's —it's —it's
            the long shot! Love My Mondays! wins by a neck!

I empty the bags
of Daddy's ashes
at the finish line

along the grandstand fences
sprinkle the winner's circle
garnish the plush geraniums

dig some ashes deep beneath
the 195-year-old Japanese white pine
shading the paddock

go home pleased
twenty dollars short
the day cleared of rain.

THOROUGHBRED

Father of stone, timber,
liquor, butter

you are my palette
of oily rainbow colors

indigo sheen
of your one black silk suit

leaf-green felt
of casino craps tables

red-and-black-checkered
gas-scented
sawdust-flecked
lumber jacket

dazzling sleek jockey shirts
urging fast thoroughbreds.

Will I see you again
my pungent, piquant hero

my crapshooter-wrecked
ship of foolish dreams

my freight
of remembrance?

AFTER THE RACES

One night after the races
he didn't return home.

Stomach ulcerated
from countless aspirin

taken daily for chronic pain
in his back and limbs.

He bled from the mouth
into the stench

of a beer-drenched elevator
at Yonkers Raceway.

He said the crowd
stepped over him.

He said
no one helped.

That night
from his hospital bed

he said
he lost his shirt.

CREEK

O Creek,

You are my counsel

You are my virtue, my sustenance

You are glimmer and brightness

You are beauty and the right to beauty

You are the flow of good fortune

You are the chance meeting taken and held

You are a cool compress
the touch of comfort upon my worries

You caress my fingers
and do not cramp the hand that directs this pen

O Creek,

I am not damaged

I am not ill fated

I am not forsaken

VI

LAMENT

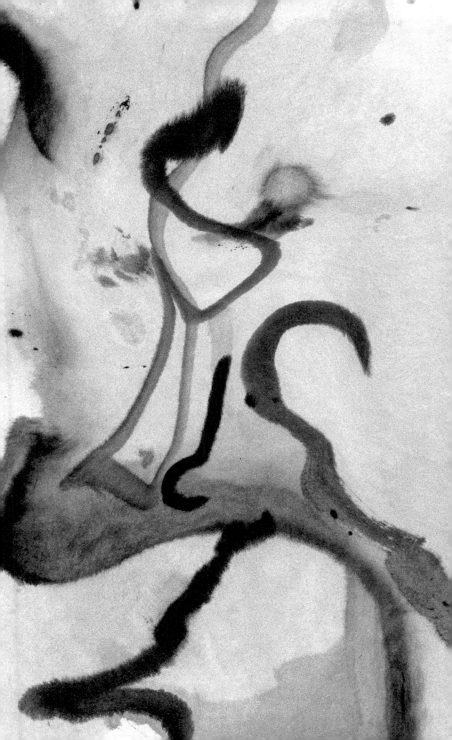

FAINT HEART

I am afraid to write

that I am afraid to write

the words I was afraid to tell you

BLADE AGAINST STEEL

Disappointments
linger like trash, Daddy,

    torn tickets
    after the horserace

    the shredded
    Daily Racing Form

    too few poker chips
    worth redeeming for cash.

Harsh memories clamber
along the texture of you

my gambling man.
Did chance betray our luck?

Are you at
heaven's gate?

Perhaps it is
a stable gate

smelling of straw
open and golden.

Do you sleep
with horses

or does your head
still hang sadly

as when you asked me
why I do not confide

and I answered
with silence?

Listen.
I will tell you.

Look back
into your little girl's eyes

the radiant wreaths
of hazel iris

the middlemost dots
of inner night.

Examine
their tenderness.

Her best brother
like an uprooted weed

bent over
your thick thighs

cries into the rose carpet
as you slap his naked ass

again and again
and she inhales the heat

of your fierce palm
upon her own neck

where it struck
shoving her headlong

into a white
blossoming hedge.

Still. Still. Still, I cannot swallow
the wounding brute of you

that bitter, errant incident
of fatherhood misguided.

A piercing siren-pitch of fear
like blade against steel

burns
                my throat
                                shut.

FUGUE

Father, a blue dot
between your eyes
the desert is silent   Father, a blue dot
       between your eyes
       you are cold   Father, a blue dot
             between your eyes
             you leave me wanting

LAMENT

His final words:

I don't know what to do

I don't know what to do

I don't know what to do

I don't know what to do

mumbled continually
from his cracked tongue
hissing lungs.

I had some ideas
mind you.

Tell your son, your pride,
his incalculable worth, your gratitude

for his many cook-nights
while you were too sick

to work the stoves
the fraught, steamy kitchen.

Your wife, sing of her unwavering partnership,
her trove of careing, trust, good sense, delight.

Savor her arms around your heft and muscle.
I color her patience Indulgent Violet

her constancy, Deep Amber
ancient as insects.

Last chance, Daddy.
Take it!

Me, tell me
you love me

with your dying breath.
Tell me you love me

without the jokey
 —just a little bit.

Say it.
I love you.

Period.

But he was busy
finding a way to leave

his hard-fought
precious life.

And I
childish to the end

eyes red
salty with grief

sat, pleading Daddy
to set free my doubts.

This decent man
of unruly passions

would have run
into a burning building for me

stopped a speeding train
a bullet

caught me
falling from a high building

without one second
of hesitation.

No. I dared not interfere
say one word aloud.

Our silence held us
as it always held us

close as my warm breath
to his parched split lips.

Your little girl
accompanies you

and your shepherd dogs
Lucky and Bingo

into the teeming landscape
of your wooded acreage.

Mother had no curiosity
for such frenzied green.

But I tell you, Daddy,
that little girl

would have chewed nails
to tend the home fires

carry water
trim candle wicks

on stormy nights
thrive there—with you—

among flowering pink dogwoods
blue flag iris   red tiger lily

> —wild man
> wild child—
>   .

DESERT

I am no longer running.
I have measured the past

measured my words
put down stakes

built a tiny home
of my own

as you built your "little joint
on the highway," Daddy.

I mirror your
three-plus lost acres

with three lots
of Southwest high desert.

House of mud
riverstone and timber

an outhouse
no well

woodstove
for warmth.

I avenge your losses
tit for tat

counter love's ambivalence
with thick sturdy walls

split wood with axe and maul
shun the hobbles of caution

parry grief with mortar
eat hot dogs, drink scotch

—you are in my blood.

I remain true to Chance
faithful to Lady Luck.

Juniper, cactus,
piñon, grow here

no mitt-leafed chestnut
no sweet-tempered pink dogwood.

I live the rugged song
of arid land

accompanied by a chorus
of scrub jays

the tympani
of August's dry thunder.

Mighty cottonwoods convene
along the low agile rivers

in autumn turn to gold
more precious than a royal flush.

Four-o'clocks mourn the evening
purple, deep as snail's blood.

Desert paintbrush charges the dust
blood color of a cock's comb.

Wild flag iris thrive mountain high
in wind-scoured June meadows

true blue to my memory of you—
live fast, lush, exuberant lives

die quietly
curled into themselves.

I inherit earth's capacious bounty
shelter in the shimmer of desert nights

constellations bear witness
to our bond, Daddy,

flesh of your flesh
father-daughter

abiding.

The epigraph is the final stanza of the final poem, "Cormorants," from Michael McGriff's extraordinary book, *Dismantling the Hills* (University of Pittsburgh Press, 2008). Used with permission of the author.

"*Tantus labor non sit cassus*"
A line from the thirteenth-century poem/hymn Dies irae, attributed to Thomas of Celano, probably older in origin, and sung at the Catholic Mass for the dead. The English gloss "so much lablor let it not be lost" is from Br.Alexis Bugnolo's translation of the poem (Franciscan archive. org/de celano/opera/diesirae.html).

"Wiccan"
The Wicca religion involves, among other things, the practice of magic. Not all wiccans practice magic, but for those who do, spiritual author and practitioner Lisa Chamberlain writes, "Magic is the art of consciously using your intent to direct the energies of nature to create a positive outcome to your life"(wiccaliving.com/what-is-magic/).

"1918. Influenza.
The 1918 influenza pandemic was severe and deadly. An estimated 500 million people were infected worldwide—one-third of the world's population. Deaths in the United States were estimated at about 675,000—(cdc.gov/flu/pandemic-resources/1918-pandemic-h1n1.html).

"striped bass"
About the Hudson river, Keven Zawacki writes, "In the 1940s, General Electric set up two plants, in Fort Edward and Hudson Falls, tasked with manufacturing electronics components. ...From 1947 to 1977, more than one million pounds of polychlorinated biphenyls, or PCBs, from those

two plants flowed into the river and downstream, contaminating the water and wildlife in its wake" ("The Story—and Fate—of the Hudson River", Westchester Magazine, March 19, 2020).

"fin"
Slang for a five-dollar bill, from the Yiddish word finf, meaning five.

"purple, deep as snail's blood"
Tyrian purple is a rare pigment made from the mucus of several species of Murex snail. Produrction began as early as 1200 BCE (Wikipedia).

"doeling"
As the experts at Roy's Farm put it, "A doeling is a female goat under one year of age, not yet sexually active. If people call a young female goat doeling, that means she is still a little girl"
(roysfarm.com/all-about-a-doeling-goat/).

ACKNOWLEDGMENTS

My deepest gratitude to my best brother, Francis, whom I grow to know, love, and admire more each year; his wife, Diana; and their terrific children, Tracey, Paul, and Jennifer. For my grandmothers Raffaella and Lucia, and Grandpa Giovanni, who is my first memory of pure delight. I am especially grateful for my parents, Teresa and Frank. Their unfailing hard work and support, their love, strength, and steadfast belief in the enduring bond of family. They are sewn into the very fiber of my being.

Thank you, friends, mentors, artists, writers, publishers, and musicians. For your belief, support, and encouragement. For your creativity, your inspiration, the brilliant help many of you provided when I was fine-tuning this manuscript, and for the purest language that musicians bring—the breath and of life's beauty.

In particular, I want to thank Alicia Allen, Ellen Bass, Francesca Belanger, Kyce Bello, Oro Lynn Benson, Monika Bittman, Sabrina Bowers, Billy Brown, Jaye Burros, Frank Cody, Deborah Cole, Gina Covina, Deanna Einspahr, Liz Esquer, Morgan Farley, Maxine Fine, Eva Fleischner, Marion-April Goering, Kerby Goforth, John Graham, Mary Harvey, Tony Hoagland, Edith Illes, Katherine Keil, Yvonne Klein, Marie Landau, Catherine Leonardo, Dana Levin, Joan Logghe, Hilary Lorenz, Mary McGinnis, Michael McGriff, Larry McLaughlin, J. B. Moore, Mary Morris, Myra Nissim, Bill Page, Manuela Paul, Anne Pearson, Lesley Poling-Kempes, Flavia Rando, Terry Rich, Zoe Robles, Barbara Rockman, Miriam Sagan, Audrey Schomer, Patricia Schott-Rower, Elke Sigal, Paul Slovak, Alice Sorensen, Eileen Sutera, Irene Talbot, Julie Thompson, Peggy Thompson, Loretta Ulmschneider, Susie Verkamp, Julie Wagner, Eleanor Walker, April Werner, Bob White, Madeline Williamson, Robert M. Wilson, Sarah Wolbach, Martha Yates, Jean Fogel Zee, Jaye Zimet, and all who share their lives, brighten the path, extend a hand, listen.

Ginger Legato is a poet, artist and book designer. Her poems have appeared in *American Tanka, Fixed and Free Poetry Anthology 2021, Heliotrope, Rubberreality, Seeds, The Magazine, Trickster,* and *Written with a Spoon: A Poet's Cookbook.* She received a First Place Award for a single poem from the New Mexico State Poetry Society and is a winner of the Southwest Literary Center/Recursos de Santa Fe, Discovery Competition.

Legato is well known as an interior book designer for the Penguin Poetry Series. She earned her BFA from the Pratt Institute, and studied sculpture at Parsons School of Design and welding at the Art Students League of New York City. Her artwork has been exhibited in New York galleries, the Brooklyn Bridge subway station, and the Brooklyn Museum. Her current work may be found on Instagram. She lives in Santa Fe, New Mexico.

The Adobe Original font Warnock began as a private font requested by Chris Warnock for his father's personal use. It was designed by award-winning long time Adobe staff designer Robert Slimbach in honor of John Warnock, the co-founder of Adobe Systems. Slimbach wanted to design a font that mirrored the visionary spirit that Warnock embodied for Adobe, and found it in this classic and yet still contemporary family of fonts.